Hey, how'd that teddy bear get stuck up in a tree?

A teddy
bear?
WHERE?

Wait, that's no teddy bear—it's a koala: a furry, tree-climbing animal that lives in Australia!

SECRET IDENTITY

When people from Europe settled in Australia centuries ago, they mistook the lovable creatures climbing in trees for a type of bear. The name "koala bear" stuck, even though koalas are actually marsupials just like several other famous Australian animals. (You'll meet them later.)

G'day,
MATE!

5

Let's take a look at a cuddly koala...

Those fluffy ears!

That snuggly body!

Those button eyes!

Let's face it:

Koalas are . . .

7

SO CUTE!

Mom always told me I was ADORABLE.

Koalas spend a big part of their lives in the treetops.

EASY CHAIR

Not only are koalas expert tree climbers, they're expert tree sitters! Koala rumps are extra furry, providing a built-in cushion for lounging in branches. Koalas in southern Australia, where it gets colder, have even thicker fur to keep cozy during the winter.

Best seat
in the
HOUSE!

Up in the branches, they munch on their favorite food: eucalyptus leaves.

Leaves again? MY FAVORITE!

SALAD BAR
Koalas don't climb eucalyptus trees just for the view. They munch on the trees one leaf at a time, eating a pound (0.5 kg) of leaves a day. That's a lot of salad!

UNHEALTHY VEGGIES
Koala digestive systems squeeze every bit of energy from eucalyptus leaves, which are actually toxic to most animals.

PICKY EATERS

Just like you might eat different foods at dinner, koalas crave variety, too. They'll climb from tree to tree to eat different varieties of eucalyptus leaves.

SUPER SMELLERS

Koalas use their superior sense of smell to seek out other tasty leaf types. A mixed menu helps keep koalas healthy.

Eucalyptus leaves don't pack much energy, so koalas take lots of naps between snacks.

Just
FIVE MORE
minutes ...

In fact, koalas snooze about 20 hours a day!

HEY! OVER HERE!

Koalas only look cuddly. These feisty animals are actually louder—and scrappier—than they look. Male koalas make a loud grunting sound—sort of like a super burp—to let female koalas know they're around. They'll bellow day or night and have been known to keep campers awake!

You mind keepin' it **DOWN?**

17

But you know what's cuter than a sleepy koala? A baby koala!

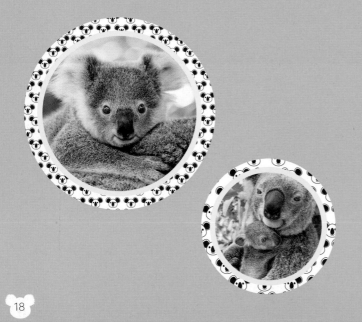
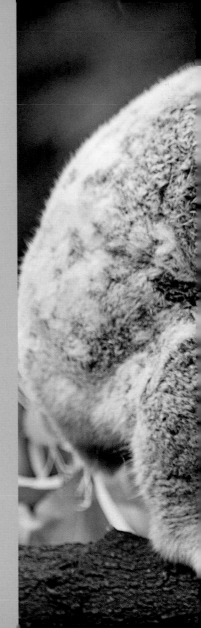

I'm called a JOEY.

19

PEEKABOO!

Koalas are teeny tiny when they're first born—they're only the size of a jelly bean! They live in a pouch on their mom until they're about six months old.

POUCH PALS

Koalas are marsupials. Marsupial babies live in their mom's pouch until they're old enough to get around on their own. Sometimes, older and younger joeys will squeeze into the same pouch. (All marsupial babies are called joeys.) Here are three other famous marsupials ...

KANGAROO
The largest and most well-known marsupial, kangaroos hop-hop-hop throughout Australia. They live in groups called mobs.

WOMBAT
The koala's closest cousin, the wombat is a tough marsupial that lives in burrows rather than tree branches.

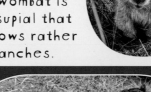

TASMANIAN DEVILS
These feisty but cute marsupials roam the forests of northwestern Tasmania, an island off Australia's coast.

When a joey outgrows the pouch, it clings to its mother's belly or back.

You're getting **HEAVY**, little one.

23

Koalas only climb down to the ground to find another tree.

KOALA RESCUE

When forest fires burn their habitat, koalas are smart enough to hide in other animals' burrows or dunk their babies in water to keep them safe. Sometimes when the fires are too severe or civilization creeps too close, koalas must be rescued and released in new forest homes.

I've got places to **GO!**

As the sun sets in the forest, we should say, **"Good night, koala."**

OH, is it your bedtime?

But we won't, because koalas are nocturnal and their day is just getting started.

CUTE AROUND THE CLOCK

Don't think koalas are lazy just because they snooze the day away. These marsupials are nocturnal, which means they keep busy climbing and eating at night. In fact, you probably look lazy to a koala because you sleep all night!

Who's
ready for
BREAKFAST?

We'll leave you
to your busy
night, koala.

MORE for
me, then!

Since 1888, the National Geographic Society has funded more than 12,000 research, exploration, and preservation projects around the world. The Society receives funds from National Geographic Partners, LLC, funded in part by your purchase. A portion of the proceeds from this book supports this vital work. To learn more, visit natgeo.com/info.

For more information, visit nationalgeographic.com, call 1-800-647-5463, or write to the following address:

National Geographic Partners
1145 17th Street N.W.
Washington, D.C. 20036-4688 U.S.A.

Visit us online at nationalgeographic.com/books

For librarians and teachers: ngchildrensbooks.org

More for kids from National Geographic: natgeokids.com

National Geographic Kids magazine inspires children to explore their world with fun yet educational articles on animals, science, nature, and more. Using fresh storytelling and amazing photography, *Nat Geo Kids* shows kids ages 6 to 14 the fascinating truth about the world—and why they should care.
kids.nationalgeographic.com/subscribe

For information about special discounts for bulk purchases, please contact National Geographic Books Special Sales: specialsales@natgeo.com

For rights or permissions inquiries, please contact National Geographic Books Subsidiary Rights: bookrights@natgeo.com

Designed by Julide Dengel
Written by Crispin Boyer

The publisher would like to thank everyone who worked to make this book come together: Rebecca Baines and Ariane Szu-Tu, editors; Shannon Hibberd, photo editor; Alix Inchausti, production editor; and Anne LeongSon and Gus Tello, design production assistants.

PHOTO CREDITS:
GI=Getty Images; MP=Minden Pictures; SS=Shutterstock
All front and back cover photos by Eric Isselee. 1, Eric Isselee/SS; 3, Roberto La Rosa/SS; 5, Jouan Rius/MP; 6, cruphoto/GI; 6-7, mauritius images GmbH/Alamy; 7, Eric Isselee/SS; 9, Jouan Rius/MP; 11, Julian W/SS; 12, I'm friday/SS; 13 (LE), Nicholas Rjabow/SS; 13 (UP), Suzi Eszterhas/MP; 13 (RT), Nicholas Rjabow/SS; 14-15 (LO RT), woodstock/SS; 16, Greg Brave/SS; 17, John Carnemolla/iStock; 18 (LE), dangdumrong/SS; 18 (RT), Suzi Eszterhas/MP; 18-19, Suzi Eszterhas/MP; 20, Suzi Eszterhas/MP; 21 (LE), Kjuuurs/Dreamstime; 21 (RT), Posnov/GI; 21 (LO), Bildagentur Zoonar GmbH/SS; 23, Klein and Hubert/MP; 24, Suzi Eszterhas/MP; 25, Mitsuaki Iwago/MP; 27, Julian Peters Photography/SS; 28, Image Source/GI; 29, Erik Veland/GI; 31, Freder/iStock/GI; 32, GlobalP/iStock/GI

Library of Congress Cataloging-in-Publication Data

Names: Boyer, Crispin, author. I National Geographic Kids (Firm), publisher. I National Geographic Society (U.S.)
Title: So cute! koalas / by Crispin Boyer.
Description: Washington, DC : National Geographic Kids, [2019] I Series: So cute! I Audience: Ages 3-7. I Audience: Pre-school, excluding K.
Identifiers: LCCN 2018035850I ISBN 9781426335273 (hardcover) I ISBN 9781426335280 (hardcover)
Subjects: LCSH: Koala--Juvenile literature.
Classification: LCC QL737.M384 B69 2019 I DDC 599.2/5--dc23
LC record available at https://lccn.loc.gov/2018035850

Printed in China
19/PPS/1

Where do joeys go to school? Elemen-tree school!